Day-By-Day Reconciliation™ Journal

A 21 day spiritual practice

by Gary Simmons, Th.D.

Published by
The Q Effect, LLC

1016 SW Lakeview Blvd
Lee's Summit, MO 64081

www.theQeffect.com

Copyright © 2004
Gary Simmons

ISBN 978-0-9824797-3-5

Printed in the USA by InstantPublisher.com

Day-By-Day Reconciliation™ Journal

A 21 day spiritual practice

Introduction

Several yours ago[1], while closing a metal garage door, I accidentally pinched my fingers in the hinges. During the seconds that followed, amidst the excruciating pain, I experienced a total life recall. Similar in many respects to a near-death experience (NDE), my lucid consciousness became preoccupied with memories of moments and circumstances when I failed to live up to my own standards of integrity, when I had inadvertently caused harm or suffering to another. After extracting my ailing hand, I became aware of an urgency to make amends and reconcile myself with those whom I had mistreated or otherwise offended.

I made a list of individuals to contact or meet and promised myself that reconciliation would be my highest priority. Within a week, I contacted everyone. Much to my surprise, everyone on my list reported that he or she had no animosity toward me and felt that whatever grievance or judgment he or she held was curiously dissolved days prior to my contact.

This unusual occurrence prompted me to investigate other NDEs to better understand and appreciate the significance of my own experience. I decided to conduct an experiment and personal study based upon my learnings. I posed the following question to myself: What would be the effect of intentionally, as a method of spiritual practice, simulating certain aspects of a near-death experience? Each night prior to going to sleep, I would practice a guided meditation ritual patterned after certain commonalities associated with NDE: having an awareness that death is imminent; being in the presence of a luminous being or divine entity; having a precise recall of past experiences with no judgment and having the awareness of the essential meaning of life; having a sense that if given the chance, I would awaken (return) with a transcendent purpose.

During the guided meditation, I imagined that it was my last night on Earth—that I would die in my sleep. As I engaged the prospects of death, I became aware of the events of my day (the recall was limited to events of the same day) and the ways my actions impacted people and situations. In the

---

[1] From The I of the Storm: Embracing Conflict, Creating Peace by Gary Simmons, published by Unity House, 2001, pages 152 – 155.

presence of Spirit, I asked that I be shown those instances where I failed to live from my highest and authentic Self, where I had acted from selfishness, indifference, or insecurity and without love, understanding, or humility. I made a list of people or situations which surfaced in my awareness and promised that if given the gift of a new day, I would make it my purpose to first reconcile myself to these before any other personal agenda item. I called the process Day-By-Day Reconciliation.

Over a period of three weeks I endeavored to practice Day-By-Day Reconciliation as a means of spiritual development, creating a new list each night and fulfilling my promise to reconcile each item the very next day, whenever possible. As a result, I observed these things: (1) reconciliation became easier with practice, as did compiling each day's list; (2) those who I presumed were offended by me appreciated my contact, and as a result, those relationships became enhanced; (3) as the practice entered the second week, those on my list reported no memory of any offense taken to begin with; (4) I also awakened *instantly* when my attitude or demeanor fell short of my standards of integrity, thereby allowing me to relate differently to the individual in the moment, and consequently, my lists became shorter and shorter until the third week, when the evening's practice produced no lists; and (5) I discovered that my *reconciliation consciousness* manifested itself as greater harmony, well-being and inner peace—both in myself and in those with whom I had difficulty. I felt healed and transformed by the practice.

While the practice seemed to accentuate a state of mindfulness throughout the day and especially during my interactions with people, the remarkable by-product of the experience was seeing and experiencing a correlation between *intentions* in consciousness and manifestations of those intentions in my outer world. Just having the *thought* of doing the right things seemed to manifest a correction in the outer. Whereas prior to a deepening of the practice, some outer action was required in order to demonstrate reconciliation consciousness, as practice deepened and intention became more authentic, the inner work produced an outer demonstration without an outer action being required.

The Day-By-Day Reconciliation Journal has been created to help you experience the power of reconciliation consciousness. At the end of your day, take time to release stress and become present and heart centered, using the following steps:

Become Heart Centered

o Find a comfortable seated position and close your eyes.

o Become aware of your breathing and feel your inhalation and exhalation. Don't try to control it, just observe it.

o If there are any thoughts, worries or concerns that are weighing on your mind, just let them go for now and know that you can pick them up later.

o Feel every part of your body, beginning with your feet, moving up through your legs and hips to the abdomen and on to the upper body. Move your awareness to your arms and hands, your shoulders, neck and head. Feel every part of your body. BE HERE NOW.

o Now shift your awareness to your heart center and breathe into your heart. Become aware of your heart energy as you breathe in and out. You may find it helpful to put your hand on your heart in order to access it.

o Continue breathing into your heart at least 10 times to focus your total awareness on your heart.

o Think of people, things and situations that you appreciate in your life. As each blessing comes into your awareness, feel your heart opening more and more.

o Let the love that is emanating from your heart fill your body.

Reflection

o In this state of peace, love and awareness, ask your heart to show you all of the instances on this day where you have fallen short of acting from your highest authentic self.

o Consider what was missing in your connection to your own sense of wholeness and worth, and had you been more heart centered how your experience would have been different.

o Now consider how you would have wanted the situation to turn out.

Journaling

o Make a list of two or three situations, as revealed to you by your heart, to revisit first thing in the morning. In these instances, the objective is to "make right" the situations, now that your heart has shown you a higher way of relating. Make a commitment to reconcile with this person before getting too caught up in the busyness of your day.

o If nothing specific is revealed, consider how you have been with yourself. Your treatment of yourself can be the focus of the journaling process. Ask your heart how to best reconcile with yourself in order to honor who and what you have come here to be.

o Include in your journaling, any aha's and insights that you notice as you practice Day-By-Day Reconciliation.

o Give thanks for the opportunity that tomorrow will bring—a wonderful gift to free yourself and someone else from the mistakes of the past.

o Record your process in the Journal each day and note any OBSERVATIONS. Keep a record of insights and learnings as your practice unfolds.

Day 1

Describe the situation revealed to you by your heart. What did or didn't you say or do that may have caused some hurt or separation?

_____

_____

_____

Ask your heart how you could have responded differently to those involved. What *difference* would you have made had you related from your heart?

_____

_____

_____

What inner resource was missing that helped create this situation? Who were you being (insecure, unworthy, not good enough, etc) instead?

_____

_____

_____

What will you do tomorrow to reconcile with the person or people in this situation. Complete the sentence:

If given the gift of tomorrow, I promise my heart that I will _____

_____

_____

_____

_____

_____

No judgment is about me.

All judgments are FOR me.

Day 1

Nothing and No one is against me

Describe the situation revealed to you by your heart. What did or didn't you say or do that may have caused some hurt or separation?

_____
_____

_____

Ask your heart how you could have responded differently to those involved. What *difference* would you have made had you related from your heart?

_____
_____

_____

What inner resource was missing that helped create this situation? Who were you being (insecure, unworthy, not good enough, etc) instead?

_____
_____

_____

What will you do tomorrow to reconcile with the person or people in this situation. Complete the sentence:

If given the gift of tomorrow, I promise my heart that I will _____

_____
_____
_____
_____
_____

Day 1

Describe the situation revealed to you by your heart. What did or didn't you say or do that may have caused some hurt or separation?

_____

_____

_____

Ask your heart how you could have responded differently to those involved. What *difference* would you have made had you related from your heart?

_____

_____

_____

What inner resource was missing that helped create this situation? Who were you being (insecure, unworthy, not good enough, etc) instead?

_____

_____

_____

What will you do tomorrow to reconcile with the person or people in this situation. Complete the sentence:

If given the gift of tomorrow, I promise my heart that I will _____

_____

_____

_____

_____

I cannot
be
diminished
when
I know my
own
worth.

OBSERVATIONS

Reflect on today's reconciliation experience. What have you discovered or learned about yourself and life so far?

_____

_____

_____

_____

_____

_____

_____

_____

_____

_____

_____

_____

_____

Day 2

Describe the situation revealed to you by your heart. What did or didn't you say or do that may have caused some hurt or separation?

_____

_____

_____

Ask your heart how you could have responded differently to those involved. What *difference* would you have made had you related from your heart?

_____

_____

_____

What inner resource was missing that helped create this situation? Who were you being (insecure, unworthy, not good enough, etc) instead?

_____

_____

_____

What will you do tomorrow to reconcile with the person or people in this situation. Complete the sentence:

If given the gift of tomorrow, I promise my heart that I will

_____

_____

_____

_____

_____

Being a victim means that you don't have to show up in your life to make the difference.

Have you ever wished your life was different?

What would be the difference you would make if it was?

You make the difference.

Change is for no other purpose.

Day 2

Describe the situation revealed to you by your heart. What did or didn't you say or do that may have caused some hurt or separation?

_____
_____
_____

Ask your heart how you could have responded differently to those involved. What *difference* would you have made had you related from your heart?

_____
_____
_____

What inner resource was missing that helped create this situation? Who were you being (insecure, unworthy, not good enough, etc) instead?

_____
_____
_____

What will you do tomorrow to reconcile with the person or people in this situation. Complete the sentence:

If given the gift of tomorrow, I promise my heart that I will _____

_____
_____
_____
_____

Day 2

Describe the situation revealed to you by your heart. What did or didn't you say or do that may have caused some hurt or separation?

_____

_____

_____

Ask your heart how you could have responded differently to those involved. What *difference* would you have made had you related from your heart?

_____

_____

_____

What inner resource was missing that helped create this situation? Who were you being (insecure, unworthy, not good enough, etc) instead?

_____

_____

_____

What will you do tomorrow to reconcile with the person or people in this situation. Complete the sentence:

If given the gift of tomorrow, I promise my heart that I will

_____

_____

_____

_____

_____

There is no spiritual principle that supports blame.

OBSERVATIONS

Reflect on today's reconciliation experience. What have you discovered or learned about yourself and life so far?

_____

_____

_____

_____

_____

_____

_____

_____

_____

_____

_____

_____

_____

Day 3

Describe the situation revealed to you by your heart. What did or didn't you say or do that may have caused some hurt or separation?

_____

_____

_____

Ask your heart how you could have responded differently to those involved. What *difference* would you have made had you related from your heart?

_____

_____

_____

What inner resource was missing that helped create this situation? Who were you being (insecure, unworthy, not good enough, etc) instead?

_____

_____

_____

What will you do tomorrow to reconcile with the person or people in this situation. Complete the sentence:

If given the gift of tomorrow, I promise my heart that I will _____

_____

_____

_____

_____

You are either the Way Of God or in the way of God.

Pick one.

18

Day 3

Wholeness
is a way of
relating
that
happens
when
you are
connected
to your
experience
and your
heart;
when you
know that
your
presence
matters;
and
when you
are being
the Way of
God.

Describe the situation revealed to you by your heart. What did or didn't you say or do that may have caused some hurt or separation?

_____

_____

_____

Ask your heart how you could have responded differently to those involved. What *difference* would you have made had you related from your heart?

_____

_____

_____

What inner resource was missing that helped create this situation? Who were you being (insecure, unworthy, not good enough, etc) instead?

_____

_____

_____

What will you do tomorrow to reconcile with the person or people in this situation. Complete the sentence:

If given the gift of tomorrow, I promise my heart that I will _____

_____

_____

_____

_____

Day 3

Describe the situation revealed to you by your heart. What did or didn't you say or do that may have caused some hurt or separation?

_____

_____

_____

Ask your heart how you could have responded differently to those involved. What *difference* would you have made had you related from your heart?

_____

_____

_____

What inner resource was missing that helped create this situation? Who were you being (insecure, unworthy, not good enough, etc) instead?

_____

_____

_____

What will you do tomorrow to reconcile with the person or people in this situation. Complete the sentence:

If given the gift of tomorrow, I promise my heart that I will _____

_____

_____

_____

_____

If you don't feel safe or okay, relax.

You're in mis-perception.

See it right before you try to make it right.

OBSERVATIONS

Reflect on today's reconciliation experience. What have you discovered or learned about yourself and life so far?

_____

_____

_____

_____

_____

_____

_____

_____

_____

_____

_____

_____

_____

Day 4

Describe the situation revealed to you by your heart. What did or didn't you say or do that may have caused some hurt or separation?

_____

_____

_____

Ask your heart how you could have responded differently to those involved. What *difference* would you have made had you related from your heart?

_____

_____

_____

What inner resource was missing that helped create this situation? Who were you being (insecure, unworthy, not good enough, etc) instead?

_____

_____

_____

What will you do tomorrow to reconcile with the person or people in this situation. Complete the sentence:

If given the gift of tomorrow, I promise my heart that I will

_____

_____

_____

_____

_____

Life is a mirror. The mirror can only reflect how we are showing up.

No amount of prayer will change the properties of the mirror.

Day 4

God has no problem with how our life looks or feels. How our life looks and feels is not against us.

Describe the situation revealed to you by your heart. What did or didn't you say or do that may have caused some hurt or separation?

_____

_____

_____

Ask your heart how you could have responded differently to those involved. What *difference* would you have made had you related from your heart?

_____

_____

_____

What inner resource was missing that helped create this situation? Who were you being (insecure, unworthy, not good enough, etc) instead?

_____

_____

_____

What will you do tomorrow to reconcile with the person or people in this situation. Complete the sentence:

If given the gift of tomorrow, I promise my heart that I will _____

_____

_____

_____

_____

_____

Day 4

Describe the situation revealed to you by your heart. What did or didn't you say or do that may have caused some hurt or separation?

_____

_____

_____

Ask your heart how you could have responded differently to those involved. What *difference* would you have made had you related from your heart?

_____

_____

_____

What inner resource was missing that helped create this situation? Who were you being (insecure, unworthy, not good enough, etc) instead?

_____

_____

_____

What will you do tomorrow to reconcile with the person or people in this situation. Complete the sentence:

If given the gift of tomorrow, I promise my heart that I will

_____

_____

_____

_____

_____

Life can
only
be against
who
you are
not.

OBSERVATIONS

Reflect on today's reconciliation experience. What have you discovered or learned about yourself and life so far?

_____

_____

_____

_____

_____

_____

_____

_____

_____

_____

_____

_____

_____

Day 5

Describe the situation revealed to you by your heart. What did or didn't you say or do that may have caused some hurt or separation?

_____

_____

_____

Ask your heart how you could have responded differently to those involved. What *difference* would you have made had you related from your heart?

_____

_____

_____

What inner resource was missing that helped create this situation? Who were you being (insecure, unworthy, not good enough, etc) instead?

_____

_____

_____

What will you do tomorrow to reconcile with the person or people in this situation. Complete the sentence:

If given the gift of tomorrow, I promise my heart that I will

_____

_____

_____

_____

_____

It is only in separating from "**who you are not**" that leads to the attainment of peace and wholeness.

Day 5

Describe the situation revealed to you by your heart. What did or didn't you say or do that may have caused some hurt or separation?

_____

_____

_____

Ask your heart how you could have responded differently to those involved. What *difference* would you have made had you related from your heart?

_____

_____

_____

What inner resource was missing that helped create this situation? Who were you being (insecure, unworthy, not good enough, etc) instead?

_____

_____

_____

What will you do tomorrow to reconcile with the person or people in this situation. Complete the sentence:

If given the gift of tomorrow, I promise my heart that I will

_____

_____

_____

_____

_____

When someone judges you... Say "tell me more."

Day 5

Describe the situation revealed to you by your heart. What did or didn't you say or do that may have caused some hurt or separation?

_____

_____

_____

Ask your heart how you could have responded differently to those involved. What *difference* would you have made had you related from your heart?

_____

_____

_____

What inner resource was missing that helped create this situation? Who were you being (insecure, unworthy, not good enough, etc) instead?

_____

_____

_____

What will you do tomorrow to reconcile with the person or people in this situation. Complete the sentence:

If given the gift of tomorrow, I promise my heart that I will

_____

_____

_____

_____

_____

The first step to wholeness is in seeing the distinction between you and your experience.

OBSERVATIONS

Reflect on today's reconciliation experience. What have you discovered or learned about yourself and life so far?

_____

_____

_____

_____

_____

_____

_____

_____

_____

_____

_____

_____

_____

Day 6

Describe the situation revealed to you by your heart. What did or didn't you say or do that may have caused some hurt or separation?

_____

_____

_____

Ask your heart how you could have responded differently to those involved. What *difference* would you have made had you related from your heart?

_____

_____

_____

What inner resource was missing that helped create this situation? Who were you being (insecure, unworthy, not good enough, etc) instead?

_____

_____

_____

What will you do tomorrow to reconcile with the person or people in this situation. Complete the sentence:

If given the gift of tomorrow, I promise my heart that I will _____

_____

_____

_____

_____

_____

Your divine inheritance is your capacity to make the difference.

Day 6

A
judgment
is never
about you.

When you
react, you
make it
about you.

Describe the situation revealed to you by your heart. What did or didn't you say or do that may have caused some hurt or separation?

_____

_____

_____

Ask your heart how you could have responded differently to those involved. What *difference* would you have made had you related from your heart?

_____

_____

_____

What inner resource was missing that helped create this situation? Who were you being (insecure, unworthy, not good enough, etc) instead?

_____

_____

_____

What will you do tomorrow to reconcile with the person or people in this situation. Complete the sentence:

If given the gift of tomorrow, I promise my heart that I will _____

_____

_____

_____

_____

_____

Day 6

Describe the situation revealed to you by your heart. What did or didn't you say or do that may have caused some hurt or separation?

_____

_____

_____

Ask your heart how you could have responded differently to those involved. What *difference* would you have made had you related from your heart?

_____

_____

_____

What inner resource was missing that helped create this situation? Who were you being (insecure, unworthy, not good enough, etc) instead?

_____

_____

_____

What will you do tomorrow to reconcile with the person or people in this situation. Complete the sentence:

If given the gift of tomorrow, I promise my heart that I will _____

_____

_____

_____

_____

The principle which governs the quality of life is:

I make my life mean what it means.

OBSERVATIONS

Reflect on today's reconciliation experience. What have you discovered or learned about yourself and life so far?

_____

_____

_____

_____

_____

_____

_____

_____

_____

_____

_____

_____

_____

Day 7

Describe the situation revealed to you by your heart. What did or didn't you say or do that may have caused some hurt or separation?

_____
_____
_____

Ask your heart how you could have responded differently to those involved. What *difference* would you have made had you related from your heart?

_____
_____
_____

What inner resource was missing that helped create this situation? Who were you being (insecure, unworthy, not good enough, etc) instead?

_____
_____
_____

What will you do tomorrow to reconcile with the person or people in this situation. Complete the sentence:

If given the gift of tomorrow, I promise my heart that I will

_____
_____
_____
_____
_____
_____

You cannot see your life without YOU in the view.

Day 7

You know
you are
lost
in the
reflection
when you
need to be
right;
need
things to
be a
certain
way;
or when
you
resist,
avoid,
or become
defensive.

Describe the situation revealed to you by your heart. What did or didn't you say or do that may have caused some hurt or separation?

_____

_____

_____

Ask your heart how you could have responded differently to those involved. What **difference** would you have made had you related from your heart?

_____

_____

_____

What inner resource was missing that helped create this situation? Who were you being (insecure, unworthy, not good enough, etc) instead?

_____

_____

_____

What will you do tomorrow to reconcile with the person or people in this situation. Complete the sentence:

If given the gift of tomorrow, I promise my heart that I will_____

_____

_____

_____

_____

_____

Day 7

Describe the situation revealed to you by your heart. What did or didn't you say or do that may have caused some hurt or separation?

_____

_____

_____

Ask your heart how you could have responded differently to those involved. What *difference* would you have made had you related from your heart?

_____

_____

_____

What inner resource was missing that helped create this situation? Who were you being (insecure, unworthy, not good enough, etc) instead?

_____

_____

_____

What will you do tomorrow to reconcile with the person or people in this situation. Complete the sentence:

If given the gift of tomorrow, I promise my heart that I will

_____

_____

_____

_____

_____

Faith is the avenue of awareness that sees as God sees.

Love is the avenue of awareness that sees all life as ONE.

OBSERVATIONS

Reflect on today's reconciliation experience. What have you discovered or learned about yourself and life so far?

_____

_____

_____

_____

_____

_____

_____

_____

_____

_____

_____

_____

_____

Day 8

Describe the situation revealed to you by your heart. What did or didn't you say or do that may have caused some hurt or separation?

_____

_____

_____

Ask your heart how you could have responded differently to those involved. What *difference* would you have made had you related from your heart?

_____

_____

_____

What inner resource was missing that helped create this situation? Who were you being (insecure, unworthy, not good enough, etc) instead?

_____

_____

_____

What will you do tomorrow to reconcile with the person or people in this situation. Complete the sentence:

If given the gift of tomorrow, I promise my heart that I will _____

_____

_____

_____

_____

The are two ways of working with challenges: Separate from what looks or feels against you. Or, separate from who you are not. Only in the latter can you find peace and healing.

Day 8

Conflict
is our
spiritual
midwife.
It brings us
into the
struggle
of
separation.

Separate
from
who you are
not to find
peace.

Describe the situation revealed to you by your heart. What did or didn't you say or do that may have caused some hurt or separation?

_____

_____

_____

Ask your heart how you could have responded differently to those involved. What ***difference*** would you have made had you related from your heart?

_____

_____

_____

What inner resource was missing that helped create this situation? Who were you being (insecure, unworthy, not good enough, etc) instead?

_____

_____

_____

What will you do tomorrow to reconcile with the person or people in this situation. Complete the sentence:

If given the gift of tomorrow, I promise my heart that I will _____

_____

_____

_____

_____

Day 8

Describe the situation revealed to you by your heart. What did or didn't you say or do that may have caused some hurt or separation?

_____

_____

_____

Ask your heart how you could have responded differently to those involved. What *difference* would you have made had you related from your heart?

_____

_____

_____

What inner resource was missing that helped create this situation? Who were you being (insecure, unworthy, not good enough, etc) instead?

_____

_____

_____

What will you do tomorrow to reconcile with the person or people in this situation. Complete the sentence:

If given the gift of tomorrow, I promise my heart that I will _____

_____

_____

_____

_____

Who have you come here to be?

OBSERVATIONS

Reflect on today's reconciliation experience. What have you discovered or learned about yourself and life so far?

_____

_____

_____

_____

_____

_____

_____

_____

_____

_____

_____

_____

_____

Day 9

Describe the situation revealed to you by your heart. What did or didn't you say or do that may have caused some hurt or separation?

_____

_____

_____

Ask your heart how you could have responded differently to those involved. What *difference* would you have made had you related from your heart?

_____

_____

_____

What inner resource was missing that helped create this situation? Who were you being (insecure, unworthy, not good enough, etc) instead?

_____

_____

_____

What will you do tomorrow to reconcile with the person or people in this situation. Complete the sentence:

If given the gift of tomorrow, I promise my heart that I will

_____

_____

_____

_____

_____

When we feel we are not enough, nothing outside of us can complete us.

Day 9

Making THE difference is our spiritual job description.

Describe the situation revealed to you by your heart. What did or didn't you say or do that may have caused some hurt or separation?

_____

_____

_____

Ask your heart how you could have responded differently to those involved. What *difference* would you have made had you related from your heart?

_____

_____

_____

What inner resource was missing that helped create this situation? Who were you being (insecure, unworthy, not good enough, etc) instead?

_____

_____

_____

What will you do tomorrow to reconcile with the person or people in this situation. Complete the sentence:

If given the gift of tomorrow, I promise my heart that I will _____

_____

_____

_____

_____

_____

Day 9

Describe the situation revealed to you by your heart. What did or didn't you say or do that may have caused some hurt or separation?

_____

_____

_____

Ask your heart how you could have responded differently to those involved. What *difference* would you have made had you related from your heart?

_____

_____

_____

What inner resource was missing that helped create this situation? Who were you being (insecure, unworthy, not good enough, etc) instead?

_____

_____

_____

What will you do tomorrow to reconcile with the person or people in this situation. Complete the sentence:

If given the gift of tomorrow, I promise my heart that I will _____

_____

_____

_____

_____

_____

Being present means being connected to your experience without pushing it away. This is the essence of non-resistance.

OBSERVATIONS

Reflect on today's reconciliation experience. What have you discovered or learned about yourself and life so far?

Day 10

Describe the situation revealed to you by your heart. What did or didn't you say or do that may have caused some hurt or separation?

_____

_____

_____

Ask your heart how you could have responded differently to those involved. What *difference* would you have made had you related from your heart?

_____

_____

_____

What inner resource was missing that helped create this situation? Who were you being (insecure, unworthy, not good enough, etc) instead?

_____

_____

_____

What will you do tomorrow to reconcile with the person or people in this situation. Complete the sentence:

If given the gift of tomorrow, I promise my heart that I will

_____

_____

_____

_____

_____

Until you realize that life is FOR you, you cannot experience your wholeness and true worth.

Day 10

Describe the situation revealed to you by your heart. What did or didn't you say or do that may have caused some hurt or separation?

_____
_____
_____

Ask your heart how you could have responded differently to those involved. What **difference** would you have made had you related from your heart?

_____
_____
_____

What inner resource was missing that helped create this situation? Who were you being (insecure, unworthy, not good enough, etc) instead?

_____
_____
_____

What will you do tomorrow to reconcile with the person or people in this situation. Complete the sentence:

If given the gift of tomorrow, I promise my heart that I will _____

_____
_____
_____
_____
_____

Make your
Path
be about
proving
nothing is
against you
and you
will
discover
what
wholeness
really is.

Day 10

Describe the situation revealed to you by your heart. What did or didn't you say or do that may have caused some hurt or separation?

_____

_____

_____

Ask your heart how you could have responded differently to those involved. What *difference* would you have made had you related from your heart?

_____

_____

_____

What inner resource was missing that helped create this situation? Who were you being (insecure, unworthy, not good enough, etc) instead?

_____

_____

_____

What will you do tomorrow to reconcile with the person or people in this situation. Complete the sentence:

If given the gift of tomorrow, I promise my heart that I will _____

_____

_____

_____

_____

_____

Insecurity and inadequacy arise out of how you are relating to your experience, not how your experience is relating to you.

OBSERVATIONS

Reflect on today's reconciliation experience. What have you discovered or learned about yourself and life so far?

_____

_____

_____

_____

_____

_____

_____

_____

_____

_____

_____

_____

_____

Day 11

Describe the situation revealed to you by your heart. What did or didn't you say or do that may have caused some hurt or separation?

_____

_____

_____

Ask your heart how you could have responded differently to those involved. What *difference* would you have made had you related from your heart?

_____

_____

_____

What inner resource was missing that helped create this situation? Who were you being (insecure, unworthy, not good enough, etc) instead?

_____

_____

_____

What will you do tomorrow to reconcile with the person or people in this situation. Complete the sentence:

If given the gift of tomorrow, I promise my heart that I will _____

_____

_____

_____

_____

You cannot experience inner peace when you are worried something isn't right in your world.

Day 11

The moment we act as if something is so, the field of infinite possibilities collapses into one inevitable happenstance.

Describe the situation revealed to you by your heart. What did or didn't you say or do that may have caused some hurt or separation?

_____

_____

_____

Ask your heart how you could have responded differently to those involved. What **difference** would you have made had you related from your heart?

_____

_____

_____

What inner resource was missing that helped create this situation? Who were you being (insecure, unworthy, not good enough, etc) instead?

_____

_____

_____

What will you do tomorrow to reconcile with the person or people in this situation. Complete the sentence:

If given the gift of tomorrow, I promise my heart that I will _____

_____

_____

_____

_____

Day 11

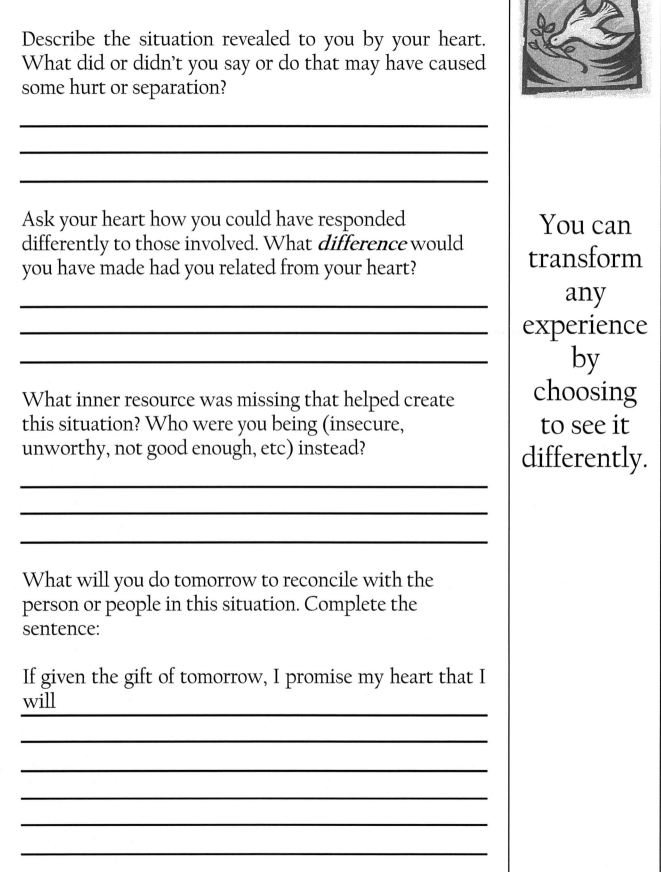

Describe the situation revealed to you by your heart. What did or didn't you say or do that may have caused some hurt or separation?

_____

_____

_____

Ask your heart how you could have responded differently to those involved. What *difference* would you have made had you related from your heart?

_____

_____

_____

What inner resource was missing that helped create this situation? Who were you being (insecure, unworthy, not good enough, etc) instead?

_____

_____

_____

What will you do tomorrow to reconcile with the person or people in this situation. Complete the sentence:

If given the gift of tomorrow, I promise my heart that I will

_____

_____

_____

_____

_____

You can transform any experience by choosing to see it differently.

OBSERVATIONS

Reflect on today's reconciliation experience. What have you discovered or learned about yourself and life so far?

_____

_____

_____

_____

_____

_____

_____

_____

_____

_____

_____

_____

_____

Day 12

Describe the situation revealed to you by your heart. What did or didn't you say or do that may have caused some hurt or separation?

_____

_____

_____

Ask your heart how you could have responded differently to those involved. What *difference* would you have made had you related from your heart?

_____

_____

_____

What inner resource was missing that helped create this situation? Who were you being (insecure, unworthy, not good enough, etc) instead?

_____

_____

_____

What will you do tomorrow to reconcile with the person or people in this situation. Complete the sentence:

If given the gift of tomorrow, I promise my heart that I will _____

_____

_____

_____

_____

Your soul moves you towards challenges because challenges stretch you in ways that help you separate from your falsehoods and dependencies.

Day 12

Ask yourself, What am I making this mean? Or, Who do I have to BE in order to have these feelings?

Describe the situation revealed to you by your heart. What did or didn't you say or do that may have caused some hurt or separation?

_____

_____

_____

Ask your heart how you could have responded differently to those involved. What *difference* would you have made had you related from your heart?

_____

_____

_____

What inner resource was missing that helped create this situation? Who were you being (insecure, unworthy, not good enough, etc) instead?

_____

_____

_____

What will you do tomorrow to reconcile with the person or people in this situation. Complete the sentence:

If given the gift of tomorrow, I promise my heart that I will _____

_____

_____

_____

_____

Day 12

Describe the situation revealed to you by your heart. What did or didn't you say or do that may have caused some hurt or separation?

_____

_____

_____

Ask your heart how you could have responded differently to those involved. What *difference* would you have made had you related from your heart?

_____

_____

_____

What inner resource was missing that helped create this situation? Who were you being (insecure, unworthy, not good enough, etc) instead?

_____

_____

_____

What will you do tomorrow to reconcile with the person or people in this situation. Complete the sentence:

If given the gift of tomorrow, I promise my heart that I will

_____

_____

_____

_____

_____

We are the Way of God when we love with the heart.

We are the Truth of God when we look with the heart.

We are the Life of God when we lead with the heart.

OBSERVATIONS

Reflect on today's reconciliation experience. What have you discovered or learned about yourself and life so far?

_____

_____

_____

_____

_____

_____

_____

_____

_____

_____

_____

_____

_____

_____

Day 13

Describe the situation revealed to you by your heart. What did or didn't you say or do that may have caused some hurt or separation?

_____

_____

_____

Ask your heart how you could have responded differently to those involved. What *difference* would you have made had you related from your heart?

_____

_____

_____

What inner resource was missing that helped create this situation? Who were you being (insecure, unworthy, not good enough, etc) instead?

_____

_____

_____

What will you do tomorrow to reconcile with the person or people in this situation. Complete the sentence:

If given the gift of tomorrow, I promise my heart that I will

_____

_____

_____

_____

_____

_____

Love, look, and lead with the heart and make the difference.

Day 13

There is a place in every relationship where mind and heart interact to create spiritual growth and transformation.

Describe the situation revealed to you by your heart. What did or didn't you say or do that may have caused some hurt or separation?

_____
_____
_____

Ask your heart how you could have responded differently to those involved. What *difference* would you have made had you related from your heart?

_____
_____
_____

What inner resource was missing that helped create this situation? Who were you being (insecure, unworthy, not good enough, etc) instead?

_____
_____
_____

What will you do tomorrow to reconcile with the person or people in this situation. Complete the sentence:

If given the gift of tomorrow, I promise my heart that I will _____

_____
_____
_____
_____

Day 13

Describe the situation revealed to you by your heart. What did or didn't you say or do that may have caused some hurt or separation?

_____

_____

_____

Ask your heart how you could have responded differently to those involved. What *difference* would you have made had you related from your heart?

_____

_____

_____

What inner resource was missing that helped create this situation? Who were you being (insecure, unworthy, not good enough, etc) instead?

_____

_____

_____

What will you do tomorrow to reconcile with the person or people in this situation. Complete the sentence:

If given the gift of tomorrow, I promise my heart that I will _____

_____

_____

_____

_____

Relating to a person or situation authentic- ally is the ultimate power that we possess.

OBSERVATIONS

Reflect on today's reconciliation experience. What have you discovered or learned about yourself and life so far?

_____

_____

_____

_____

_____

_____

_____

_____

_____

_____

_____

_____

_____

Day 14

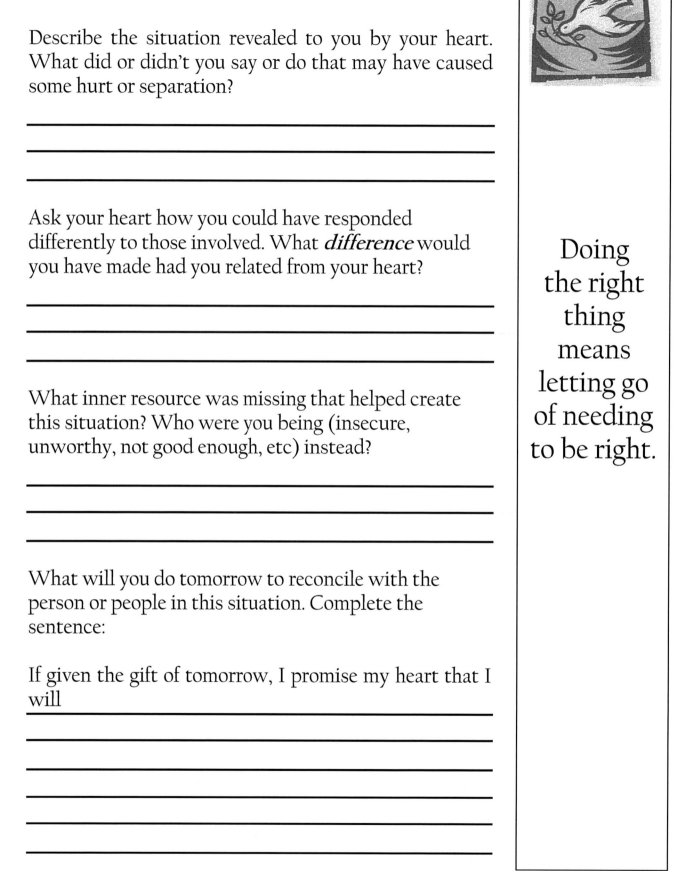

Describe the situation revealed to you by your heart. What did or didn't you say or do that may have caused some hurt or separation?

_____

_____

_____

Ask your heart how you could have responded differently to those involved. What *difference* would you have made had you related from your heart?

_____

_____

_____

What inner resource was missing that helped create this situation? Who were you being (insecure, unworthy, not good enough, etc) instead?

_____

_____

_____

What will you do tomorrow to reconcile with the person or people in this situation. Complete the sentence:

If given the gift of tomorrow, I promise my heart that I will _____

_____

_____

_____

_____

Doing the right thing means letting go of needing to be right.

Day 14

Blessing your enemy helps you dismantle the belief that the enemy is against you.

Your enemy can only be against who you are not.

Describe the situation revealed to you by your heart. What did or didn't you say or do that may have caused some hurt or separation?

_____

_____

_____

Ask your heart how you could have responded differently to those involved. What *difference* would you have made had you related from your heart?

_____

_____

_____

What inner resource was missing that helped create this situation? Who were you being (insecure, unworthy, not good enough, etc) instead?

_____

_____

_____

What will you do tomorrow to reconcile with the person or people in this situation. Complete the sentence:

If given the gift of tomorrow, I promise my heart that I will _____

_____

_____

_____

_____

Day 14

Describe the situation revealed to you by your heart. What did or didn't you say or do that may have caused some hurt or separation?

_____

_____

_____

Ask your heart how you could have responded differently to those involved. What *difference* would you have made had you related from your heart?

_____

_____

_____

What inner resource was missing that helped create this situation? Who were you being (insecure, unworthy, not good enough, etc) instead?

_____

_____

_____

What will you do tomorrow to reconcile with the person or people in this situation. Complete the sentence:

If given the gift of tomorrow, I promise my heart that I will _____

_____

_____

_____

_____

_____

Prayer helps you fill in the gaps in your awareness of God's presence and purpose in the situation.

OBSERVATIONS

Reflect on today's reconciliation experience. What have you discovered or learned about yourself and life so far?

_____ .

_____

_____

_____

_____

_____

_____

_____

_____

_____

_____

_____

_____

Day 15

Describe the situation revealed to you by your heart. What did or didn't you say or do that may have caused some hurt or separation?

_____
_____
_____

Ask your heart how you could have responded differently to those involved. What *difference* would you have made had you related from your heart?

_____
_____
_____

What inner resource was missing that helped create this situation? Who were you being (insecure, unworthy, not good enough, etc) instead?

_____
_____
_____

What will you do tomorrow to reconcile with the person or people in this situation. Complete the sentence:

If given the gift of tomorrow, I promise my heart that I will

_____
_____
_____
_____
_____
_____

When what we do is rooted in feelings of fear or inadequacy we are not moving in the direction of Spirit.

Day 15

Authenti-city supports right action and ownership of your creative process.

Who have you come here to be, and what is yours to do?

Describe the situation revealed to you by your heart. What did or didn't you say or do that may have caused some hurt or separation?

_____

_____

_____

Ask your heart how you could have responded differently to those involved. What *difference* would you have made had you related from your heart?

_____

_____

_____

What inner resource was missing that helped create this situation? Who were you being (insecure, unworthy, not good enough, etc) instead?

_____

_____

_____

What will you do tomorrow to reconcile with the person or people in this situation. Complete the sentence:

If given the gift of tomorrow, I promise my heart that I will _____

_____

_____

_____

_____

Day 15

Describe the situation revealed to you by your heart. What did or didn't you say or do that may have caused some hurt or separation?

_____

_____

_____

Ask your heart how you could have responded differently to those involved. What *difference* would you have made had you related from your heart?

_____

_____

_____

What inner resource was missing that helped create this situation? Who were you being (insecure, unworthy, not good enough, etc) instead?

_____

_____

_____

What will you do tomorrow to reconcile with the person or people in this situation. Complete the sentence:

If given the gift of tomorrow, I promise my heart that I will _____

_____

_____

_____

_____

God needs you to be who you really are because who you are is what makes you real.

OBSERVATIONS

Reflect on today's reconciliation experience. What have you discovered or learned about yourself and life so far?

_____

_____

_____

_____

_____

_____

_____

_____

_____

_____

_____

_____

_____

Day 16

Describe the situation revealed to you by your heart. What did or didn't you say or do that may have caused some hurt or separation?

_____

_____

_____

Ask your heart how you could have responded differently to those involved. What *difference* would you have made had you related from your heart?

_____

_____

_____

What inner resource was missing that helped create this situation? Who were you being (insecure, unworthy, not good enough, etc) instead?

_____

_____

_____

What will you do tomorrow to reconcile with the person or people in this situation. Complete the sentence:

If given the gift of tomorrow, I promise my heart that I will

_____

_____

_____

_____

_____

Conflict does not come to us, it comes from us.

Day 16

Describe the situation revealed to you by your heart. What did or didn't you say or do that may have caused some hurt or separation?

_____
_____
_____

Ask your heart how you could have responded differently to those involved. What **difference** would you have made had you related from your heart?

_____
_____
_____

What inner resource was missing that helped create this situation? Who were you being (insecure, unworthy, not good enough, etc) instead?

_____
_____
_____

What will you do tomorrow to reconcile with the person or people in this situation. Complete the sentence

If given the gift of tomorrow, I promise my heart that I will _____

_____
_____
_____
_____

Resistance
and
defensive-
ness
arise out of
those parts
of
ourselves
that are
not
connected
to
our
wholeness.

Day 16

Describe the situation revealed to you by your heart. What did or didn't you say or do that may have caused some hurt or separation?

_____

_____

_____

Ask your heart how you could have responded differently to those involved. What *diffeence* would you have made had you related from yourheart?

_____

_____

_____

What inner resource was missing that heled create this situation? Who were you being (inseare, unworthy, not good enough, etc) instead?

_____

_____

_____

What will you do tomorrow to reconcile wh the person or people in this situation. Complethe sentence:

If given the gift of tomorrow, I promise my krt that I will _____

_____

_____

_____

_____

_____

Conflict leads to rebirth and transformation. It is only in the presence of challenging circumstances that we awaken to the possibilities of the moment.

OBSERVATIONS

Reflect on today's reconciliation experience. What have you discovered or learned about yourself and life so far?

_____

_____

_____

_____

_____

_____

_____

_____

_____

_____

_____

_____

_____

Day 17

Describe the situation revealed to you by your heart. What did or didn't you say or do that may have caused some hurt or separation?

_____

_____

_____

Ask your heart how you could have responded differently to those involved. What *difference* would you have made had you related from your heart?

_____

_____

_____

What inner resource was missing that helped create this situation? Who were you being (insecure, unworthy, not good enough, etc) instead?

_____

_____

_____

What will you do tomorrow to reconcile with the person or people in this situation. Complete the sentence:

If given the gift of tomorrow, I promise my heart that I will

_____

_____

_____

_____

_____

When you disagree, but are willing to under-stand what is underlying the disagree-ment, you strengthen the relation-ship.

Day 17

Your soul moves you toward the present moment so you can take authentic action.

Describe the situation revealed to you by your heart. What did or didn't you say or do that may have caused some hurt or separation?

_____

_____

_____

Ask your heart how you could have responded differently to those involved. What *difference* would you have made had you related from your heart?

_____

_____

_____

What inner resource was missing that helped create this situation? Who were you being (insecure, unworthy, not good enough, etc) instead?

_____

_____

_____

What will you do tomorrow to reconcile with the person or people in this situation. Complete the sentence:

If given the gift of tomorrow, I promise my heart that I will _____

_____

_____

_____

_____

_____

Day 17

Describe the situation revealed to you by your heart. What did or didn't you say or do that may have caused some hurt or separation?

_____

_____

_____

Ask your heart how you could have responded differently to those involved. What *difference* would you have made had you related from your heart?

_____

_____

_____

What inner resource was missing that helped create this situation? Who were you being (insecure, unworthy, not good enough, etc) instead?

_____

_____

_____

What will you do tomorrow to reconcile with the person or people in this situation. Complete the sentence:

If given the gift of tomorrow, I promise my heart that I will

_____

_____

_____

_____

_____

_____

The problem with resistance is that we personalize it. We take it as evidence that someone is against us.

OBSERVATIONS

Reflect on today's reconciliation experience. What have you discovered or learned about yourself and life so far?

_____

_____

_____

_____

_____

_____

_____

_____

_____

_____

_____

_____

_____

_____

Day 18

Describe the situation revealed to you by your heart. What did or didn't you say or do that may have caused some hurt or separation?

_____
_____
_____

Ask your heart how you could have responded differently to those involved. What *difference* would you have made had you related from your heart?

_____
_____
_____

What inner resource was missing that helped create this situation? Who were you being (insecure, unworthy, not good enough, etc) instead?

_____
_____
_____

What will you do tomorrow to reconcile with the person or people in this situation. Complete the sentence:

If given the gift of tomorrow, I promise my heart that I will_____

_____
_____
_____
_____

You cannot hear another person unless you possess the capacity to be changed by what someone says.

The change is about moving from separation to co-creation.

Day 18

If you feel diminished by what someone says to you, you have not really heard what is being said.

Listen with your heart, not your head.

Describe the situation revealed to you by your heart. What did or didn't you say or do that may have caused some hurt or separation?

_____
_____
_____

Ask your heart how you could have responded differently to those involved. What **difference** would you have made had you related from your heart?

_____
_____
_____

What inner resource was missing that helped create this situation? Who were you being (insecure, unworthy, not good enough, etc) instead?

_____
_____
_____

What will you do tomorrow to reconcile with the person or people in this situation. Complete the sentence:

If given the gift of tomorrow, I promise my heart that I will _____
_____
_____
_____
_____

Day 18

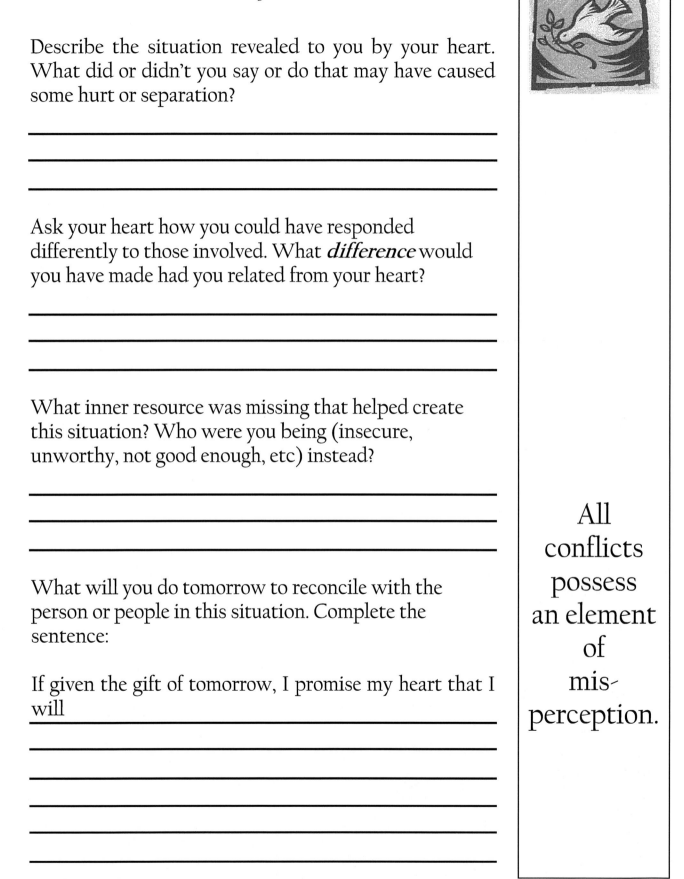

Describe the situation revealed to you by your heart. What did or didn't you say or do that may have caused some hurt or separation?

_____

_____

_____

Ask your heart how you could have responded differently to those involved. What *difference* would you have made had you related from your heart?

_____

_____

_____

What inner resource was missing that helped create this situation? Who were you being (insecure, unworthy, not good enough, etc) instead?

_____

_____

_____

What will you do tomorrow to reconcile with the person or people in this situation. Complete the sentence:

If given the gift of tomorrow, I promise my heart that I will _____

_____

_____

_____

_____

_____

All conflicts possess an element of mis-perception.

OBSERVATIONS

Reflect on today's reconciliation experience. What have you discovered or learned about yourself and life so far?

_____

_____

_____

_____

_____

_____

_____

_____

_____

_____

_____

_____

_____

Day 19

Describe the situation revealed to you by your heart. What did or didn't you say or do that may have caused some hurt or separation?

_____

_____

_____

Ask your heart how you could have responded differently to those involved. What *difference* would you have made had you related from your heart?

_____

_____

_____

What inner resource was missing that helped create this situation? Who were you being (insecure, unworthy, not good enough, etc) instead?

_____

_____

_____

What will you do tomorrow to reconcile with the person or people in this situation. Complete the sentence:

If given the gift of tomorrow, I promise my heart that I will _____

_____

_____

_____

_____

There is only one relationship. Your Relationship with God.

When you experience God in your relationship with life, others, and yourself, you have attained communion.

Day 19

When you
cannot see
God in
your
life
situation
you
become
fearful.

Describe the situation revealed to you by your heart. What did or didn't you say or do that may have caused some hurt or separation?

_____

_____

_____

Ask your heart how you could have responded differently to those involved. What *difference* would you have made had you related from your heart?

_____

_____

_____

What inner resource was missing that helped create this situation? Who were you being (insecure, unworthy, not good enough, etc) instead?

_____

_____

_____

What will you do tomorrow to reconcile with the person or people in this situation. Complete the sentence:

If given the gift of tomorrow, I promise my heart that I will_____

_____

_____

_____

_____

_____

Day 19

Describe the situation revealed to you by your heart. What did or didn't you say or do that may have caused some hurt or separation?

_____

_____

_____

Ask your heart how you could have responded differently to those involved. What *difference* would you have made had you related from your heart?

_____

_____

_____

What inner resource was missing that helped create this situation? Who were you being (insecure, unworthy, not good enough, etc) instead?

_____

_____

_____

What will you do tomorrow to reconcile with the person or people in this situation. Complete the sentence:

If given the gift of tomorrow, I promise my heart that I will_____

_____

_____

_____

_____

_____

Abundance is another word for I AM.

Lack only exists in context with the meaning you attribute to what you have or have not.

OBSERVATIONS

Reflect on today's reconciliation experience. What have you discovered or learned about yourself and life so far?

_____

_____

_____

_____

_____

_____

_____

_____

_____

_____

_____

_____

_____

Day 20

Describe the situation revealed to you by your heart. What did or didn't you say or do that may have caused some hurt or separation?

_____

_____

_____

Ask your heart how you could have responded differently to those involved. What *difference* would you have made had you related from your heart?

_____

_____

_____

What inner resource was missing that helped create this situation? Who were you being (insecure, unworthy, not good enough, etc) instead?

_____

_____

_____

What will you do tomorrow to reconcile with the person or people in this situation. Complete the sentence:

If given the gift of tomorrow, I promise my heart that I will _____

_____

_____

_____

_____

You are the Truth of God when you are a witness to the activity of presence of God in the situation.

Day 20

You cannot be centered or present to your life experience unless you are connected to your heart.

Describe the situation revealed to you by your heart. What did or didn't you say or do that may have caused some hurt or separation?

_____
_____
_____

Ask your heart how you could have responded differently to those involved. What *difference* would you have made had you related from your heart?

_____
_____
_____

What inner resource was missing that helped create this situation? Who were you being (insecure, unworthy, not good enough, etc) instead?

_____
_____
_____

What will you do tomorrow to reconcile with the person or people in this situation. Complete the sentence:

If given the gift of tomorrow, I promise my heart that I will _____

_____
_____
_____
_____

Day 20

Describe the situation revealed to you by your heart. What did or didn't you say or do that may have caused some hurt or separation?

_____

_____

_____

Ask your heart how you could have responded differently to those involved. What *difference* would you have made had you related from your heart?

_____

_____

_____

What inner resource was missing that helped create this situation? Who were you being (insecure, unworthy, not good enough, etc) instead?

_____

_____

_____

What will you do tomorrow to reconcile with the person or people in this situation. Complete the sentence:

If given the gift of tomorrow, I promise my heart that I will_____

_____

_____

_____

_____

Peace-making is about creating a pathway to God.

OBSERVATIONS

Reflect on today's reconciliation experience. What have you discovered or learned about yourself and life so far?

_____

_____

_____

_____

_____

_____

_____

_____

_____

_____

_____

_____

_____

_____

Day 21

Describe the situation revealed to you by your heart. What did or didn't you say or do that may have caused some hurt or separation?

_____

_____

_____

Ask your heart how you could have responded differently to those involved. What *difference* would you have made had you related from your heart?

_____

_____

_____

What inner resource was missing that helped create this situation? Who were you being (insecure, unworthy, not good enough, etc) instead?

_____

_____

_____

What will you do tomorrow to reconcile with the person or people in this situation. Complete the sentence:

If given the gift of tomorrow, I promise my heart that I will _____

_____

_____

_____

_____

You are here to make the difference.

What would be the **difference** you would make if you knew in your heart that nothing and no one is against you?

Day 21

You don't have enough time to fix yourself.

You can make the difference because "who you have come here to be" is what the world needs NOW.

Describe the situation revealed to you by your heart. What did or didn't you say or do that may have caused some hurt or separation?

_____

_____

_____

Ask your heart how you could have responded differently to those involved. What *difference* would you have made had you related from your heart?

_____

_____

_____

What inner resource was missing that helped create this situation? Who were you being (insecure, unworthy, not good enough, etc) instead?

_____

_____

_____

What will you do tomorrow to reconcile with the person or people in this situation. Complete the sentence:

If given the gift of tomorrow, I promise my heart that I will _____

_____

_____

_____

_____

Day 21

Describe the situation revealed to you by your heart. What did or didn't you say or do that may have caused some hurt or separation?

_____

_____

_____

Ask your heart how you could have responded differently to those involved. What *difference* would you have made had you related from your heart?

_____

_____

_____

What inner resource was missing that helped create this situation? Who were you being (insecure, unworthy, not good enough, etc) instead?

_____

_____

_____

What will you do tomorrow to reconcile with the person or people in this situation. Complete the sentence:

If given the gift of tomorrow, I promise my heart that I will _____

_____

_____

_____

_____

_____

The key is knowing who you have come here to be,

and that your presence matters,

and that you are the Way of God.

OBSERVATIONS

Reflect on today's reconciliation experience. What have you discovered or learned about yourself and life so far?

_____

_____

_____

_____

_____

_____

_____

_____

_____

_____

_____

_____

_____

You Make THE Difference

We know that your practice of Day-By-Day Reconciliation has changed your life. Tell us your story of how this practice has impacted your life and your relationship to others. With your permission, portions of your contribution may be included in our upcoming book. You may use the space below to write your narrative and mail to:

revjane@imakethedifference.net

_____

_____

_____

_____

_____

_____

_____

_____

_____

_____

_____

_____